Holy the Firm

ANNIE DILLARD

Holy the Firm

HARPER COLOPHON BOOKS
Harper & Row, Publishers
New York, Cambridge, Philadelphia, San Francisco
London, Mexico City, São Paulo, Sydney

242

D

A hardcover edition of this book was published by Harper & Row, Publishers, Inc.

A portion of this work originally appeared in *Harper's Magazine*.

HOLY THE FIRM. Copyright © 1977 by Annie Dillard. All rights reserved. Printed in the United States of America. No part of this book may be used or reproduced in any manner whatsoever without written permission except in the case of brief quotations embodied in critical articles and reviews. For information address Harper & Row, Publishers, Inc., 10 East 53rd Street, New York, N.Y. 10022. Published simultaneously in Canada by Fitzhenry & Whiteside Limited, Toronto.

First HARPER COLOPHON edition published 1984.

Designed by Gloria Adelson

Library of Congress Cataloging in Publication Data

Dillard, Annie.
  Holy the firm.

  1. Meditations. I. Title.
BV4832.2.D54   1977   242   77-6883
ISBN 0-06-091098-4 (pbk.)

84 85 86 87 88 10 9 8 7 6 5 4 3 2

for Gary

PART ONE

Newborn and Salted

Every day is a god, each day is a god, and holiness
holds forth in time. I worship each god, I praise
each day splintered down, splintered down and
wrapped in time like a husk, a husk of many colors
spreading, at dawn fast over the mountains split.

I wake in a god. I wake in arms holding my quilt,
holding me as best they can inside my quilt.

Someone is kissing me—already. I wake, I cry

"Oh," I rise from the pillow. Why should I open my eyes?

I open my eyes. The god lifts from the water. His head fills the bay. He is Puget Sound, the Pacific; his breast rises from pastures; his fingers are firs; islands slide wet down his shoulders. Islands slip blue from his shoulders and glide over the water, the empty, lighted water like a stage.

Today's god rises, his long eyes flecked in clouds. He flings his arms, spreading colors; he arches, cupping sky in his belly; he vaults, vaulting and spread, holding all and spread on me like skin.

Under the quilt in my knees' crook is a cat. She wakes; she curls to bite her metal sutures. The day is real; already, I can feel it click, hear it clicking under my knees.

The day is real; the sky clicks securely in place over the mountains, locks round the islands, snaps slap on the bay. Air fits flush on farm roofs; it rises inside the doors of barns and rubs at yellow barn windows. Air clicks up my hand cloven into fingers and wells in my ears' holes, whole and entire. I call it simplicity, the way matter is smooth and alone.

I toss the cat. I stand and smooth the quilt. "Oh," I cry, "Oh!"

I live on northern Puget Sound, in Washington State, alone. I have a gold cat, who sleeps on my legs, named Small. In the morning I joke to her blank face, Do you remember last night? Do you remember? I throw her out before breakfast, so I can eat.

There is a spider, too, in the bathroom, with whom I keep a sort of company. Her little outfit always reminds me of a certain moth I helped to kill. The spider herself is of uncertain lineage, bulbous at the abdomen and drab. Her six-inch mess of a web works, works somehow, works miraculously, to keep her alive and me amazed. The web itself is in a corner behind the toilet, connecting tile wall to tile wall and floor, in a place where there is, I would have thought, scant traffic. Yet under the web are sixteen or so corpses she has tossed to the floor.

The corpses appear to be mostly sow bugs, those little armadillo creatures who live to travel flat out in houses, and die round. There is also a new shred of earwig, three old spider skins crinkled and clenched, and two moth bodies, wingless and huge and empty, moth bodies I drop to my knees to see.

Today the earwig shines darkly and gleams, what there is of him: a dorsal curve of thorax and abdomen, and a smooth pair of cerci by which I knew his name. Next week, if the other bodies are any indication, he will be shrunken and gray, webbed to the floor with dust. The sow bugs beside him are hollow and empty of color, fragile, a breath away from brittle fluff. The spider skins lie on their sides, translucent and ragged, their legs drying in knots. And the moths, the empty moths, stagger against each other, headless, in a confusion of arcing strips of chitin like peeling varnish, like a jumble of buttresses for cathedral domes, like nothing resembling moths, so that I should hesitate to call them moths, except that I have had some experience with the figure Moth reduced to a nub.

Two summers ago I was camping alone in the Blue Ridge Mountains in Virginia. I had hauled myself and gear up there to read, among other things, James Ramsey Ullman's *The Day on Fire*, a novel about Rimbaud that had made me want to be a writer when I was sixteen; I was hoping it would do it again. So I read, lost, every day sitting under a tree by my tent, while warblers swung in the leaves overhead and bristle worms trailed their inches over the twiggy dirt at my feet; and I read every night by candlelight, while barred owls called in the forest and pale moths massed round my head in the clearing, where my light made a ring.

Moths kept flying into the candle. They would hiss and recoil, lost upside down in the shadows among my cooking pans. Or they would singe their wings and fall, and their hot wings, as if melted, would stick to the first thing they touched—a pan, a lid, a spoon—so that the snagged moths could flutter only in tiny arcs, unable to struggle free. These I could release by a quick flip with a stick; in the morning I would find my cooking stuff gilded with torn flecks of moth wings, triangles of shiny dust here and there on the aluminum. So I read, and boiled water, and replenished candles, and read on.

One night a moth flew into the candle, was caught, burnt dry, and held. I must have been staring at the candle, or maybe I looked up when a shadow crossed my page; at any rate, I saw it all. A golden female moth, a biggish one with a two-inch wingspan, flapped into the fire, dropped her abdomen into the wet wax, stuck, flamed, frazzled and fried in a second. Her moving wings ignited like tissue paper, enlarging the circle of light in the clearing and creating out of the darkness the sudden blue sleeves of my sweater, the green leaves of jewelweed by my side, the ragged red trunk of a pine. At once the light contracted again and the moth's wings vanished in a fine, foul smoke. At the same time her six legs clawed, curled, blackened, and ceased, disappearing utterly. And her head jerked in spasms, making a spattering noise; her antennae crisped and burned away and her heaving mouth parts crackled like pistol fire. When it was all over, her head was, so far as I could determine, gone, gone the long way of her wings and legs. Had she been new, or old? Had she mated and laid her eggs, had she done her work? All that was left was the glowing horn shell of her abdomen and thorax— a fraying, partially collapsed gold tube jammed upright in the candle's round pool.

And then this moth-essence, this spectacular skeleton, began to act as a wick. She kept burning. The wax rose in the moth's body from her soaking abdomen to her thorax to the jagged hole where her head should be, and widened into flame, a saffron-yellow flame that robed her to the ground like any immolating monk. That candle had two wicks, two flames of identical height, side by side. The moth's head was fire. She burned for two hours, until I blew her out.

She burned for two hours without changing, without bending or leaning—only glowing within, like a building fire glimpsed through silhouetted walls, like a hollow saint, like a flame-faced virgin gone to God, while I read by her light, kindled, while Rimbaud in Paris burnt out his brains in a thousand poems, while night pooled wetly at my feet.

And that is why I believe those hollow crisps on the bathroom floor are moths. I think I know moths, and fragments of moths, and chips and tatters of utterly empty moths, in any state. How many of you, I asked the people in my class, which of you want to give your lives and be writers? I was trembling from coffee, or cigarettes, or the closeness of faces all around me. (Is this what we live for? I thought; is this the only final beauty: the color of any skin in any light, and living, human eyes?) All hands rose to the question. (You, Nick? Will you? Margaret? Randy? Why do I want them to mean it?) And then I tried to tell them what the choice must mean: you can't be anything else. You must go at your life with a broadax. . . . They had no idea what I was saying. (I have two hands, don't I? And all this energy, for as long as I can remember. I'll do it in the evenings, after skiing, or on the way home from the bank, or after the children are asleep. . . .) They thought I was raving again. It's just as well.

I have three candles here on the table which I disentangle from the plants and light when visitors come. Small usually avoids them, although once she came too close and her tail caught fire; I rubbed it out before she noticed. The flames move light over everyone's skin, draw light to the surface of the faces of my friends. When the people leave I never blow the candles out, and after I'm asleep they flame and burn.

The Cascade range, in these high latitudes, backs almost into the water. There is only a narrow strip, an afterthought of foothills and farms sixty miles wide, between the snowy mountains and the sea. The mountains wall well. The rest of the country—most of the rest of the planet, in some very real sense, excluding a shred of British Columbia's coastline and the Alaskan islands—is called, and profoundly felt to be, simply "East of the Mountains." I've been there.

I came here to study hard things—rock mountain and salt sea—and to temper my spirit on their edges. "Teach me thy ways, O Lord" is, like all prayers, a rash one, and one I cannot but recommend. These mountains—Mount Baker and the Sisters and Shuksan, the Canadian Coastal Range and the

Olympics on the peninsula—are surely the edge of the known and comprehended world. They are high. That they bear their own unimaginable masses and weathers aloft, holding them up in the sky for anyone to see plain, makes them, as Chesterton said of the Eucharist, only the more mysterious by their very visibility and absence of secrecy. They are the western rim of the real, if not considerably beyond it. If the Greeks had looked at Mount Baker all day, their large and honest art would have broken, and they would have gone fishing, as these people do. And as perhaps I one day shall.

But the mountains are, incredibly, east. When I first came here I faced east and watched the mountains, thinking, These are the Ultima Thule, the final westering, the last serrate margin of time. Since they are, incredibly, east, I must be no place at all. But the sun rose over the snowfields and woke me where I lay, and I rose and cast a shadow over someplace, and thought, There is, God help us, more. So gathering my bowls and spoons, and turning my head, as it were, I moved to face west, relinquishing all hope of sanity, for what is more.

And what is more is islands: sea, and unimaginably solid islands, and sea, and a hundred rolling skies. You spill your breath. Nothing holds; the whole show rolls. I can imagine Virginias no less than Pacifics. Inland valley, pool, desert, plain—it's all a falling sheaf of edges, like a quick-flapped deck of cards, like a dory or a day launched all unchristened, lost at sea. Land is a poured thing and time a surface film lapping and fringeing at fastness, at a hundred hollow and receding blues. Breathe fast: we're backing off the rim.

Here is the fringey edge where elements meet and realms mingle, where time and eternity spatter each other with foam. The salt sea and the islands, molding and molding, row upon rolling row, don't quit, nor do winds end nor skies cease from spreading in curves. The actual percentage of land mass to sea in the Sound equals that of the rest of the planet: we have less time than we knew. Time is eternity's pale interlinear, as the islands are the sea's. We have less time than we knew and that time buoyant, and cloven, lucent, and missile, and wild.

The room where I live is plain as a skull, a firm

setting for windows. A nun lives in the fires of the spirit, a thinker lives in the bright wick of the mind, an artist lives jammed in the pool of materials. (Or, a nun lives, thoughtful and tough, in the mind, a nun lives, with that special poignancy peculiar to religious, in the exile of materials; and a thinker, who would think of something, lives in the clash of materials, and in the world of spirit where all long thoughts must lead; and an artist lives in the mind, that warehouse of forms, and an artist lives, of course, in the spirit. So.) But this room is a skull, a fire tower, wooden, and empty. Of itself it is nothing, but the view, as they say, is good.

Since I live in one room, one long wall of which is glass, I am myself, at everything I do, a backdrop to all the landscape's occasions, to all its weathers, colors and lights. From the kitchen sink, and from my bed, and from the table, the couch, the hearth, and the desk, I see land and water, islands, sky.

The land is complex and shifting: the eye leaves it. There is a white Congregationalist church among Douglas firs; there is a green pasture between two yellow fallow fields; there are sheep bent over

beneath some alders, and beside them a yard of
running brown hens. But everything in the landscape
points to sea. The land's progress of colors leads the
eye up a distant hill, a sweeping big farm of a hill
whose yellow pastures bounce light all day from a
billion stems and blades; and down the hill's rim drops
a dark slope of fir forest, a slant your eye rides down
to the point, the dark sliver of land that holds the bay.
From this angle you see the bay cut a crescent; your
eye flies up the black beach to the point, or slides down
the green firs to the point, and the point is an arrow
pointing over and over, with its log-strewn beach,
its gray singleness, and its recurved white edging of
foam, to sea: to the bright sound, the bluing of water
with distance at the world's rim, and on it the far
blue islands, and over these lights the light clouds.

You can't picture it, can you? Neither can I. Oh,
the desk is yellow, the oak table round, the ferns
alive, the mirror cold, and I never have cared. I read.
In the Middle Ages, I read, "the idea of a thing
which a man framed for himself was always more real
to him than the actual thing itself." Of course. I am

in my Middle Ages; the world at my feet, the world through the window, is an illuminated manuscript whose leaves the wind takes, one by one, whose painted illuminations and halting words draw me, one by one, and I am dazzled in days and lost.

There is, in short, one country, one room, one enormous window, one cat, one spider, and one person: but I am hollow. And, for now, there are the many gods of mornings and the many things to give them for their work—lungs and heart, muscle, nerve, and bone—and there is the no man's land of many things wherein they dwell, and from which I seek to call them, in work that's mine.

Nothing is going to happen in this book. There is only a little violence here and there in the language, at the corner where eternity clips time.

So I read. Armenians, I read, salt their newborn babies. I check somewhere else: so did the Jews at the time of the prophets. They washed a baby in water, salted him, and wrapped him in cloths. When God promised to Aaron and all the Levites all the offerings

Israel made to God, the firstfruits and the firstling livestock, "all the best of the oil, and all the best of the wine," he said of this promise, "It is a covenant of salt forever." In the Roman church baptism, the priest places salt in the infant's mouth.

I salt my breakfast eggs. All day long I feel created. I can see the blown dust on the skin on the back of my hand, the tiny trapezoids of chipped clay, moistened and breathed alive. There are some created sheep in the pasture below me, sheep set down here precisely, just touching their blue shadows hoof to hoof on the grass. Created gulls pock the air, rip great curved seams in the settled air: I greet my created meal, amazed.

I have been drawing a key to the islands I see from my window. Everyone told me a different set of names for them, until one day a sailor came and named them all with such authority that I believed him. So I penciled an outline of the horizon on a sheet of paper and labeled the lobes: Skipjack, Sucia, Saturna, Salt Spring, Bare Island. . . .

Today, November 18 and no wind, today a veil of

air has lifted that I didn't know was there. I see a
new island, a new wrinkle, the deepening of wonder,
behind the blue translucence the sailor said is Salt
Spring Island. I have no way of learning its name.
I bring the labeled map to the table and pencil a new
line. Call that: Unknown Island North; Water-
Statue; Sky-Ruck; Newborn and Salted; Waiting
for Sailor.

Henry Miller relates that Knut Hamsun once said,
in response to a questionnaire, that he wrote to kill
time. This is funny in a number of ways. In a number
of ways I kill myself laughing, looking out at islands.
Startled, the yellow cat on the floor stares over her
shoulder. She has carried in a wren, I suddenly
see, a wren she has killed, whose dead wings point
askew on the circular rug. It is time. Out with you
both. I'm busy laughing, to kill time. I shoo the cat
from the door, turn the wren over in my palm,
unmoved, and drop him from the porch, down to
the winterkilled hair grass and sedge, where the cat
may find him if she will, or crows, or beetles, or rain.
   When I next look up from my coffee, there is a

ruckus on the porch. The cat has dragged in a god, scorched. He is alive. I run outside. Save for his wings, he is a perfect, very small man. He is fair, thin-skinned in the cat's mouth, and kicking. His hair is on fire and stinks; his wingtips are blackened and seared. From the two soft flaps of the cat's tiger muzzle his body jerks, naked. One of his miniature hands pushes hard at her nose. He waves his thighs; he beats her face and the air with his smoking wings. I cannot breathe. I run at the cat to scare her; she drops him, casting at me an evil look, and runs from the porch.

The god lies gasping and perfect. He is no longer than my face. Quickly I snuff the smoldering fire in his yellow hair with a finger and thumb. In so doing I accidentally touch his skull, brush against his hot skull, which is the size of a hazelnut, as the saying goes, warm-skinned and alive.

He rolls his colorless eyes toward mine: his long wings catch strength from the sun, and heave.

Later I am walking in the day's last light. The god rides barefoot on my shoulder, or astride it, or tugging or swinging on loops of my hair.

He is whistling at my ear; he is blowing a huge tune in my ear, a myth about November. He is heaping a hot hurricane into my ear, into my hair, an ignorant ditty calling things real, calling islands out of the sea, calling solid moss from curling rock, and ducks down the sky for the winter.

I see it! I see it all! Two islands, twelve islands, worlds, gather substance, gather the blue contours of time, and array themselves down distance, mute and hard.

I seem to see a road; I seem to be on a road, walking. I seem to walk on a blacktop road that runs over a hill. The hill creates itself, a powerful suggestion. It creates itself, thickening with apparently solid earth and waving plants, with houses and browsing cattle, unrolling wherever my eyes go, as though my focus were a brush painting in a world. I cannot escape the illusion. The colorful thought persists, this world, a dream forced into my ear and sent round my body on ropes of hot blood. If I throw my eyes past the rim of the hill to see the real—stars, were they? something with wings, or loops?—I elaborate the illusion instead; I rough in a middle ground. I stitch the transparent curtain solid with bright phantom mountains, with thick clouds gliding just so over their shadows on green water, with blank, impenetrable sky. The dream fills in, like wind widening over a bay. Quickly I look to the flat dream's rim for a glimpse of that old deep . . . and, just as quickly, the blue slaps shut, the colors wrap everything out. There is not a chink. The sky is gagging on trees. I seem to be on a road, walking, greeting the hedgerows, the rose hips, apples, and thorn. I seem to be on a road walking, familiar with neighbors, high-handed with cattle, smelling the sea, and alone. Already, I know the names of things. I can kick a stone.

Time is enough, more than enough, and matter multiple and given. The god of today is a child, a baby new and filling the house, remarkably here in the flesh. He is day. He thrives in a cup of wind, landlocked and thrashing. He unrolls, revealing his shape an edge at a time, a smatter of content, footfirst: a word, a friend for coffee, a windshift, the shingling or coincidence of ideas. Today, November 18 and no wind, is clear. Terry Wean—who fishes, and takes my poetry course—could see Mount Rainier. He hauls his reef net gear from the bay; we talk on its deck while he hammers at shrunken knots. The Moores for dinner. In bed, I call to me my sad cat, I read. Like a rug or wrap rolling unformed up a loom, the day discovers itself, like the poem.

The god of today is rampant and drenched. His arms spread, bearing moist pastures; his fingers spread, fingering the shore. He is time's live skin; he burgeons up from day like any tree. His legs spread crossing the heavens, flicking hugely, and flashing and arcing around the earth toward night.

This is the one world, bound to itself and exultant. It fizzes up in trees, trees heaving up streams of salt to their leaves. This is the one air, bitten by grackles; time is alone and in and out of mind. The god of today is a boy, pagan and fernfoot. His power is enthusiasm; his innocence is mystery. He sockets into everything that is, and that right holy. Loud as music, filling the grasses and skies, his day spreads rising at

home in the hundred senses. He rises, new and
surrounding; he *is* everything that is, wholly here
and emptied—flung, and flowing, sowing, unseen,
and flown.

PART TWO

God's Tooth

Into this world falls a plane.

The earth is a mineral speckle planted in trees. The plane snagged its wing on a tree, fluttered in a tiny arc, and struggled down.

I heard it go. The cat looked up. There was no reason: the plane's engine simply stilled after takeoff, and the light plane failed to clear the firs. It fell easily; one wing snagged on a fir top; the metal fell down

35

the air and smashed in the thin woods where cattle browse; the fuel exploded; and Julie Norwich seven years old burnt off her face.

Little Julie mute in some room at St. Joe's now, drugs dissolving into the sheets. Little Julie with her eyes naked and spherical, baffled. Can you scream without lips? Yes. But do children in long pain scream?

It is November 19 and no wind, and no hope of heaven, and no wish for heaven, since the meanest of people show more mercy than hounding and terrorist gods.

The airstrip, a cleared washboard affair on the flat crest of a low hill, is a few long fields distant from my house—up the road and through the woods, or across the sheep pasture and through the woods. A flight instructor told me once that when his students get cocky, when they think they know how to fly a plane, he takes them out here and makes them land on that field. You go over the wires and down, and along the strip and up before the trees, or vice versa, vice versa, depending on the wind. But the airstrip is not unsafe. Jesse's engine failed. The FAA will cart the wreckage away, bit by bit, picking it out of the tree trunk, and try to discover just why that engine failed. In the meantime, the emergency siren has sounded, causing everyone who didn't see the plane go down to halt—Patty at her weaving, Jonathan slicing apples, Jan washing her baby's face—to halt, in pity and terror, wondering which among us got hit, by what bad accident, and why. The volunteer firemen have mustered; the fire trucks have come—stampeding Shuller's sheep—and gone, bearing burnt Julie and Jesse her father to the emergency room in town, leaving the rest of us to gossip, fight grass fires on the airstrip, and pray, or wander from window to window, fierce.

So she is burnt on her face and neck, Julie Norwich. The one whose teeth are short in a row, Jesse and Ann's oldest, red-kneed, green-socked, carrying cats.

I saw her only once. It was two weeks ago, under an English hawthorn tree, at the farm.

There are many farms in this neck of the woods, but only one we call "the farm"—the old Corcoran place, where Gus grows hay and raises calves: the farm, whose abandoned frame chicken coops ply the fields like longboats, like floating war canoes; whose clay driveway and grass footpaths are a tangle of orange calendula blossoms, ropes, equipment, and seeding grasses; the farm, whose canny heifers and bull calves figure the fences, run amok to the garden, and plant themselves suddenly black and white, up to their necks in green peas.

Between the gray farmhouse and the barn is the green grass farmyard, suitable for all projects. That day, sixteen of us were making cider. It was cold. There were piles of apples everywhere. We had filled our trucks that morning, climbing trees and shaking their boughs, dragging tarps heavy with apples, hauling bushels and boxes and buckets of apples, and loading them all back to the farm. Jesse and Ann, who are in their thirties, with Julie and the baby, whose name I forget, had driven down from the mountains that morning with a truckload of apples, loose, to make cider with us, fill their jugs, and drive back. I had not met them before. We all drank coffee on the farmhouse porch to warm us; we hosed jugs in the yard. Now we were throwing apples into a shredder and wringing the mash through pillowcases, staining our palms and freezing our fingers, and decanting the pails into seventy one-gallon jugs. And all this long day, Julie Norwich chased my cat Small around the farmyard and played with her, manhandled her, next to the porch under the hawthorn tree.

She was a thin child, pointy-chinned, yellow bangs and braids. She squinted, and when you looked at her she sometimes started laughing, as if you had surprised her at using some power she wasn't yet ready to show. I kept my eye on her, wondering if she was cold with her sweater unbuttoned and bony knees bare.

She would hum up a little noise for half-hour stretches. In the intervals, for maybe five minutes each, she was trying, very quietly, to learn to whistle. I think. Or she was practicing a certain concentrated face. But I think she was trying to learn to whistle, because sometimes she would squeak a little falsetto note through an imitation whistle hole in her lips, as if that could fool anyone. And all day she was dressing and undressing the yellow cat, sticking it into a black dress, a black dress long and full as a nun's.

I was amazed at that dress. It must have been some sort of doll clothing she had dragged with her in the truck; I've never seen its kind before or since. A white collar bibbed the yoke of it like a guimpe. It had great black sleeves like wings. Julie scooped up the cat and rammed her into the cloth. I knew how she felt, exasperated, breaking her heart on a finger curl's width of skinny cat arm. I knew the many feelings she had sticking those furry arms through the sleeves. Small is not large: her limbs feel like bird bones strung in a sock. When Julie had the cat dressed in its curious habit, she would rock it like a baby doll. The cat blinked, upside down.

Once she whistled at it, or tried, blowing in its face; the cat poured from her arms and ran. It leapt across the driveway, lightfoot in its sleeves; its black dress pulled this way and that, dragging dust, bent up in back by its yellow tail. I was squeezing one end of a twisted pillowcase full of apple mash and looking over my shoulder. I watched the cat hurdle the driveway and vanish under the potting shed, cringing; I watched Julie dash after it without hesitation, seize it, hit its face, and drag it back to the tree, carrying it caught fast by either forepaw, so its body hung straight from its arms.

She saw me watching her and we exchanged a look, a very conscious and self-conscious look—because we look a bit alike and we both knew it; because she was still short and I grown; because I was stuck kneeling before the cider pail, looking at her sidewise over my shoulder; because she was carrying the cat so oddly, so that she had to walk with her long legs parted; because it was my cat, and she'd dressed it, and it looked like a nun; and because she knew I'd been watching her, and how fondly, all along. We were laughing.

We *looked* a bit alike. Her face is slaughtered now, and I don't remember mine. It is the best joke there is, that we are here, and fools—that we are sown into time like so much corn, that we are souls sprinkled at random like salt into time and dissolved here, spread into matter, connected by cells right down to our feet, and those feet likely to fell us over

a tree root or jam us on a stone. The joke part is
that we forget it. Give the mind two seconds alone
and it thinks it's Pythagoras. We wake up a hundred
times a day and laugh.

The joke of the world is less like a banana peel than
a rake, the old rake in the grass, the one you step
on, foot to forehead. It all comes together. In a
twinkling. You have to admire the gag for its
symmetry, accomplishing all with one right angle, the
same right angle which accomplishes all philosophy.
One step on the rake and it's mind under matter
once again. You wake up with a piece of tree in your
skull. You wake up with fruit on your hands. You
wake up in a clearing and see yourself, ashamed.
You see your own face and it's seven years old and
there's no knowing why, or where you've been since.
We're tossed broadcast into time like so much grass,
some ravening god's sweet hay. You wake up and a
plane falls out of the sky.

That day was a god, too, the day we made cider
and Julie played under the hawthorn tree. He must
have been a heyday sort of god, a husbandman. He was

spread under gardens, sleeping in time, an innocent
old man scratching his head, thinking of pruning the
orchard, in love with families.

Has he no power? Can the other gods carry time
and its loves upside down like a doll in their
blundering arms? As though we the people were
playing house—when we are serious and do love—
and not the gods? No, that day's god has no power.
No gods have power to save. There are only days.
The one great god abandoned us to days, to time's
tumult of occasions, abandoned us to the gods of days
each brute and amok in his hugeness and idiocy.

Jesse her father had grabbed her clear of the plane
this morning, and was hauling her off when the fuel
blew. A gob of flung ignited vapor hit her face, or
something flaming from the plane or fir tree hit her
face. No one else was burned, or hurt in any way.

So this is where we are. Ashes, ashes, all fall down.
How could I have forgotten? Didn't I see the heavens
wiped shut just yesterday, on the road walking?
Didn't I fall from the dark of the stars to these
senselit and noisome days? The great ridged granite

millstone of time is illusion, for only the good is real;
the great ridged granite millstone of space is illusion,
for God is spirit and worlds his flimsiest dreams: but
the illusions are almost perfect, are apparently perfect
for generations on end, and the pain is also, and
undeniably, real. The pain within the millstones'
pitiless turning is real, for our love for each other—
for world and all the products of extension—is real,
vaulting, insofar as it is love, beyond the plane of the
stones' sickening churn and arcing to the realm of
spirit bare. And you can get caught holding one end
of a love, when your father drops, and your mother;
when a land is lost, or a time, and your friend blotted
out, gone, your brother's body spoiled, and cold, your
infant dead, and you dying: you reel out love's long
line alone, stripped like a live wire loosing its sparks
to a cloud, like a live wire loosed in space to longing
and grief everlasting.

I sit at the window. It is a fool's lot, this sitting
always at windows spoiling little blowy slips of
paper and myself in the process. Shall I be old? Here
comes Small, old sparrow-mouth, wanting my lap.
Done. Do you have any earthly idea how young I am?

Where's your dress, kitty? I suppose I'll outlive this wretched cat. Get another. Leave it my silver spoons, like old ladies you hear about. I prefer dogs.

So I read. Angels, I read, belong to nine different orders. Seraphs are the highest; they are aflame with love for God, and stand closer to him than the others. Seraphs love God; cherubs, who are second, possess perfect knowledge of him. So love is greater than knowledge; how could I have forgotten? The seraphs are born of a stream of fire issuing from under God's throne. They are, according to Dionysius the Areopagite, "all wings," having, as Isaiah noted, six wings apiece, two of which they fold over their eyes. Moving perpetually toward God, they perpetually praise him, crying Holy, Holy, Holy. . . . But, according to some rabbinic writings, they can sing only the first "Holy" before the intensity of their love ignites them again and dissolves them again, perpetually, into flames. "Abandon everything," Dionysius told his disciple. "God despises ideas."

God despises everything, apparently. If he abandoned us, slashing creation loose at its base from any roots in the real; and if we in turn abandon everything—all these illusions of time and space and lives—in order to love only the real: then where are we? Thought itself is impossible, for subject can have no guaranteed connection with object, nor any object with God. Knowledge is impossible. We are precisely nowhere, sinking on an entirely imaginary ice floe, into entirely imaginary seas themselves adrift. Then we reel out love's long line alone toward a God less lovable than a grasshead, who treats us less well than we treat our lawns.

Of faith I have nothing, only of truth: that this one God is a brute and traitor, abandoning us to time, to necessity and the engines of matter unhinged. This is no leap; this is evidence of things seen: one Julie, one sorrow, one sensation bewildering the heart, and enraging the mind, and causing me to look at the world stuff appalled, at the blithering rock of trees in a random wind, at my hand like some gibberish sprouted, my fist opening and closing, so that I think, Have I once turned my hand in this circus, have I ever called it home?

Faith would be that God is self-limited utterly by his creation—a contraction of the scope of his will; that he bound himself to time and its hazards and haps as a man would lash himself to a tree for love. That God's works are as good as we make them. That God is helpless, our baby to bear, self-abandoned on the doorstep of time, wondered at by cattle and oxen. Faith would be that God moved and moves once and for all and "down," so to speak, like a diver, like a man who eternally gathers himself for a dive and eternally is diving, and eternally splitting the spread of the water, and eternally drowned.

Faith would be, in short, that God has any willful connection with time whatsoever, and with us. For I know it as given that God is all good. And I take it also as given that whatever he touches has meaning, if only in his mysterious terms, the which I readily grant. The question is, then, whether God touches anything. Is anything firm, or is time on the loose? Did Christ descend once and for all to no purpose, in a kind of divine and kenotic suicide, or ascend once and for all, pulling his cross up after him like a rope

ladder home? Is there—even if Christ holds the tip
of things fast and stretches eternity clear to the dim
souls of men—is there no link at the base of things,
some kernel or air deep in the matrix of matter from
which universe furls like a ribbon twined into time?

Has God a hand in this? Then it is a good hand.
But has he a hand at all? Or is he a holy fire burning
self-contained for power's sake alone? Then he knows
himself blissfully as flame unconsuming, as all
brilliance and beauty and power, and the rest of us
can go hang. Then the accidental universe spins mute,
obedient only to its own gross terms, meaningless,
out of mind, and alone. The universe is neither
contingent upon nor participant in the holy, in being
itself, the real, the power play of fire. The universe
is illusion merely, not one speck of it real, and we are
not only its victims, falling always into or smashed
by a planet slung by its sun—but also its captives,
bound by the mineral-made ropes of our senses.

But how do we know—how could we know—that
the real is there? By what freak chance does the skin
of illusion ever split, and reveal to us the real, which
seems to know us by name, and by what freak chance

and why did the capacity to prehend it evolve?

I sit at the window, chewing the bones in my
wrist. Pray for them: for Julie, for Jesse her father,
for Ann her mother, pray. Who will teach us to
pray? The god of today is a glacier. We live in his
shifting crevasses, unheard. The god of today is
delinquent, a barn-burner, a punk with a pittance of
power in a match. It is late, a late time to be living.
Now it is afternoon; the sky is appallingly clear.
Everything in the landscape points to sea, and the sea
is nothing; it is snipped from the real as a stuff without
form, rising up the sides of islands and falling,
mineral to mineral, salt.

Everything I see—the water, the log-wrecked
beach, the farm on the hill, the bluff, the white church
in the trees—looks overly distinct and shining. (What
is the relationship of color to this sun, of sun to
anything else?) It all looks staged. It all looks brittle
and unreal, a skin of colors painted on glass, which
if you prodded it with a finger would powder and
fall. A blank sky, perfectly blended with all other
sky, has sealed over the crack in the world where
the plane fell, and the air has hushed the matter up.

If days are gods, then gods are dead, and artists
pyrotechnic fools. Time is a hurdy-gurdy, a lampoon,
and death's a bawd. We're beheaded by the nick of
time. We're logrolling on a falling world, on time
released from meaning and rolling loose, like one of
Atalanta's golden apples, a bauble flung and forgotten,
lapsed, and the gods on the lam.

And now outside the window, deep on the horizon,
a new thing appears, as if we needed a new thing.
It is a new land blue beyond islands, hitherto hidden
by haze and now revealed, and as dumb as the rest. I
check my chart, my amateur penciled sketch of the
skyline. Yes, this land is new, this spread blue spark
beyond yesterday's new wrinkled line, beyond the
blue veil a sailor said was Salt Spring Island. How
long can this go on? But let us by all means extend
the scope of our charts.

I draw it as I seem to see it, a blue chunk fitted
just so beyond islands, a wag of graphite rising just
here above another anonymous line, and here meeting
the slope of Salt Spring: though whether this be
headland I see or heartland, or the distance-blurred

bluffs of a hundred bays, I have no way of knowing,
or if it be island or main. I call it Thule, O Julialand,
Time's Bad News; I name it Terror, the Farthest
Limb of the Day, God's Tooth.

PART THREE

Holy the Firm

I know only enough of God to want to worship
him, by any means ready to hand. There is an
anomalous specificity to all our experience in space,
a scandal of particularity, by which God burgeons
up or showers down into the shabbiest of occasions,
and leaves his creation's dealings with him in the
hands of purblind and clumsy amateurs. This is all we
are and all we ever were; God *kann nicht anders.*

This process in time is history; in space, at such shocking random, it is mystery.

A blur of romance clings to our notions of "publicans," "sinners," "the poor," "the people in the marketplace," "our neighbors," as though of course God should reveal himself, if at all, to these simple people, these Sunday school watercolor figures, who are so purely themselves in their tattered robes, who are single in themselves, while we now are various, complex, and full at heart. We are busy. So, I see now, were they. Who shall ascend into the hill of the Lord? or who shall stand in his holy place? There is no one but us. There is no one to send, nor a clean hand, nor a pure heart on the face of the earth, nor in the earth, but only us, a generation comforting ourselves with the notion that we have come at an awkward time, that our innocent fathers are all dead—as if innocence had ever been—and our children busy and troubled, and we ourselves unfit, not yet ready, having each of us chosen wrongly, made a false start, failed, yielded to impulse and the tangled comfort of pleasures, and grown exhausted, unable to seek the thread, weak, and involved. But there is no one but us. There never has been. There have been generations which remembered, and generations which forgot; there has never been a generation of whole men and women who lived well for even one day. Yet some have imagined well, with honesty and art, the detail of such a life, and have described it with such grace, that we mistake vision for history, dream for description, and fancy that life has devolved. So. You learn this studying any history at all, especially the lives of artists and visionaries; you learn it from Emerson, who noticed that the meanness of our days is itself worth our thought; and you learn it, fitful in your pew, at church.

There is one church here, so I go to it. On Sunday mornings I quit the house and wander down the hill to the white frame church in the firs. On a big Sunday there might be twenty of us there; often I am the only person under sixty, and feel as though I'm on an archaeological tour of Soviet Russia. The members are of mixed denominations; the minister is a Congregationalist, and wears a white shirt. The man knows God. Once, in the middle of the long

pastoral prayer of intercession for the whole world—
for the gift of wisdom to its leaders, for hope and
mercy to the grieving and pained, succor to the
oppressed, and God's grace to all—in the middle of
this he stopped, and burst out, "Lord, we bring you
these same petitions every week." After a shocked
pause, he continued reading the prayer. Because of
this, I like him very much. "Good morning!" he says
after the first hymn and invocation, startling me
witless every time, and we all shout back, "Good
morning!"

The churchwomen all bring flowers for the altar;
they haul in arrangements as big as hedges, of wayside
herbs in season, and flowers from their gardens,
huge bunches of foliage and blossoms as tall as I am,
in vases the size of tubs, and the altar still looks
empty, irredeemably linoleum, and beige. We had a
wretched singer once, a guest from a Canadian
congregation, a hulking blond girl with chopped hair
and big shoulders, who wore tinted spectacles and a
long lacy dress, and sang, grinning, to faltering
accompaniment, an entirely secular song about
mountains. Nothing could have been more apparent

than that God loved this girl; nothing could more surely convince me of God's unending mercy than the continued existence on earth of the church.

The higher Christian churches—where, if anywhere, I belong—come at God with an unwarranted air of professionalism, with authority and pomp, as though they knew what they were doing, as though people in themselves were an appropriate set of creatures to have dealings with God. I often think of the set pieces of liturgy as certain words which people have successfully addressed to God without their getting killed. In the high churches they saunter through the liturgy like Mohawks along a strand of scaffolding who have long since forgotten their danger. If God were to blast such a service to bits, the congregation would be, I believe, genuinely shocked. But in the low churches you expect it any minute. This is the beginning of wisdom.

Today is Friday, November 20. Julie Norwich is in the hospital, burned; we can get no word of her condition. People released from burn wards, I read once, have a very high suicide rate. They had not realized, before they were burned, that life could include such suffering, nor that they personally could be permitted such pain. No drugs ease the pain of third-degree burns, because burns destroy skin: the drugs simply leak into the sheets. His disciples asked Christ about a roadside beggar who had been blind from birth, "Who did sin, this man or his parents, that he was born blind?" And Christ, who spat on the ground, made a mud of his spittle and clay, plastered the mud over the man's eyes, and gave him sight, answered, "Neither hath this man sinned, nor his parents: but that the works of God should be made manifest in him." Really? If we take this answer to refer to the affliction itself—and not the subsequent cure—as "God's works made manifest," then we have, along with "Not as the world gives do I give unto you," two meager, baffling, and infuriating answers to one of the few questions worth asking, to wit, What in the Sam Hill is going on here?

The works of God made manifest? Do we really need more victims to remind us that we're all victims? Is this some sort of parade for which a conquering army shines up its terrible guns and rolls them up and down the streets for the people to see? Do we need blind men stumbling about, and little flamefaced children, to remind us what God can—and will—do?

I am drinking boiled coffee and watching the bay from the window. Almost all of the people who reef net have hauled their gears for the winter; the salmon runs are over, days are short. Still, boats come and go on the water—tankers, tugs and barges, rowboats and sails. There are killer whales if you're lucky, rafts of harlequin ducks if you're lucky, and every day the scoter and the solitary grebes. How many tons of sky can I see from the window? It is morning: morning! and the water clobbered with light. Yes, in fact, we do. We do need reminding, not of what God can do, but of what he cannot do, or will not, which is to catch time in its free fall and stick a nickel's worth of sense into our days. And we need reminding of what time can do, must only do; churn out enormity at random and beat it, with God's blessing, into our heads: that we are created, *created*, sojourners in a land we did not make, a land with no meaning of itself and no meaning we can make for it alone. Who are we to demand explanations of God? (And what monsters of perfection should we be if we did not?) We forget ourselves, picnicking; we forget where we are. There is no such thing as a freak accident. "God is at home," says Meister Eckhart, "We are in the far country."

We are most deeply asleep at the switch when we fancy we control any switches at all. We sleep to time's hurdy-gurdy; we wake, if we ever wake, to the silence of God. And then, when we wake to the deep shores of light uncreated, then when the dazzling dark breaks over the far slopes of time, then it's time to toss things, like our reason, and our will; then it's time to break our necks for home.

There are no events but thoughts and the heart's hard turning, the heart's slow learning where to love and whom. The rest is merely gossip, and tales for other times. The god of today is a tree. He is a forest of trees or a desert, or a wedge from wideness down to a scatter of stars, stars like salt low and dumb and abiding. Today's god said: shed. He peels from eternity always, spread; he winds into time like a rind. I am or seem to be on a road walking. The hedges are just where they were. There is a corner, and a long hill, a glimpse of snow on the mountains, a slope planted in apple trees, and a store next to a pasture, where I am going to buy the communion wine.

How can I buy the communion wine? Who am I to buy the communion wine? Someone has to buy the communion wine. Having wine instead of grape juice was my idea, and of course I offered to buy it. Shouldn't I be wearing robes and, especially, a mask? Shouldn't I *make* the communion wine? Are there holy grapes, is there holy ground, is anything here holy? There are no holy grapes, there is no holy ground, nor is there anyone but us. I have an empty knapsack over my parka's shoulders; it is cold, and I'll want my hands in my pockets. According to the Rule of St. Benedict, I should say, Our hands in our pockets. "All things come of thee, O Lord, and of thine own have we given thee." There must be a rule for the purchase of communion wine. "Will that be cash, or charge?" All I know is that when I go to this store—to buy eggs, or sandpaper, broccoli, wood screws, milk—I like to tease a bit, if he'll let me, with the owners' son, two, whose name happens to be Chandler, and who himself likes to play in the big bins of nails.

And so, forgetting myself, thank God: Hullo. Hullo, short and relatively new. Welcome again to the land of the living, to time, this hill of beans. Chandler will have, as usual, none of it. He keeps his mysterious counsel. And I'm out on the road again walking, my right hand forgetting my left. I'm out on the road again walking, and toting a backload of God.

Here is a bottle of wine with a label, Christ with a cork. I bear holiness splintered into a vessel, very God of very God, the sempiternal silence personal and brooding, bright on the back of my ribs. I start up the hill.

The world is changing. The landscape begins to respond as a current upwells. It is starting to clack with itself, though nothing moves in space and there's no wind. It is starting to utter its infinite particulars, each overlapping and lone, like a hundred hills of hounds all giving tongue. The hedgerows are blackberry brambles, white snowberries, red rose hips, gaunt and clattering broom. Their leafless stems are starting to live visibly deep in their centers, as hidden as banked fires live, and as clearly as recognition, mute, shines forth from eyes. Above me the mountains are raw nerves, sensible and exultant; the trees, the grass, and the asphalt below me are living petals of mind, each sharp and invisible, held in a greeting or glance full perfectly formed. There is something stretched or jostling about the sky which, when I study it, vanishes. Why are there all these apples in the world, and why so wet and transparent? Through all my clothing, through the pack on my back and through the bottle's glass I feel the wine. Walking faster and faster, weightless, I feel the wine. It sheds light in slats through my rib cage, and fills the buttressed vaults of my ribs with light pooled and buoyant. I am moth; I am light. I am prayer and I can hardly see.

Each thing in the world is translucent, even the cattle, and moving, cell by cell. I remember this reality. Where has it been? I sail to the crest of the hill as

if blown up the slope of a swell. I see, blasted, the
bay transfigured below me, the saltwater bay, far
down the hill past the road to my house, past the firs
and the church and the sheep in the pasture: the bay
and the islands on fire and boundless beyond it,
catching alight the unraveling sky. Pieces of the
sky are falling down. Everything, everything, is
whole, and a parcel of everything else. I myself am
falling down, slowly, or slowly lifting up. On the bay's
stone shore are people among whom I float, real
people, gathering of an afternoon, in the cells of whose
skin stream thin colored waters in pieces which give
back the general flame.

Christ is being baptized. The one who is Christ is
there, and the one who is John, and the dim other
people standing on cobbles or sitting on beach logs
back from the bay. These are ordinary people—if I
am one now, if those are ordinary sheep singing a
song in the pasture.

The two men are bare to the waist. The one walks
him into the water, and holds him under. His hand
is on his neck. Christ is coiled and white under the
water, standing on stones.

He lifts from the water. Water beads on his shoulders. I see the water in balls as heavy as planets, a billion beads of water as weighty as worlds, and he lifts them up on his back as he rises. He stands wet in the water. Each one bead is transparent, and each has a world, or the same world, light and alive and apparent inside the drop: it is all there ever could be, moving at once, past and future, and all the people. I can look into any sphere and see people stream past me, and cool my eyes with colors and the sight of the world in spectacle perishing ever, and ever renewed. I do; I deepen into a drop and see all that time contains, all the faces and deeps of the worlds and all the earth's contents, every landscape and room, everything living or made or fashioned, all past and future stars, and especially faces, faces like the cells of everything, faces pouring past me talking, and going, and gone. And I am gone.

For outside it is bright. The surface of things outside the drops has fused. Christ himself and the others, and the brown warm wind, and hair, sky, the beach, the shattered water—all this has fused. It is the one glare of holiness; it is bare and unspeakable. There is no speech nor language; there is nothing, no one thing, nor motion, nor time. There is only this everything. There is only this, and its bright and multiple noise.

I seem to be on a road, standing still. It is the top of the hill. The hedges are here, subsiding. My hands are in my pockets. There is a bottle of wine on my back, a California red. I see my feet. I move down the hill toward home.

You must rest now. I cannot rest you. For me there is, I am trying to tell you, no time.

There are a thousand new islands today, uncharted. They are salt stones on fire and dimming; I read by their light. Small the cat lies on my neck. In the bathroom the spider is working on yesterday's moth.

Esoteric Christianity, I read, posits a substance. It is a created substance, lower than metals and minerals on a "spiritual scale," and lower than salts and earths, occurring beneath salts and earths in the waxy deepness of planets, but never on the surface of planets where men could discern it; and it is in touch with the Absolute, at base. In touch with the Absolute! At base. The name of this substance is: Holy the Firm.

Holy the Firm: and is Holy the Firm in touch with metals and minerals? With salts and earths? Of course, and straight on up, till "up" ends by curving back. Does something that touched something that touched Holy the Firm in touch with the Absolute at base seep into ground water, into grain; are islands rooted in it, and trees? Of course.

Scholarship has long distinguished between two strains of thought which proceed in the West from human knowledge of God. In one, the ascetic's metaphysic, the world is far from God. Emanating from God, and linked to him by Christ, the world is yet infinitely other than God, furled away from him like the end of a long banner falling. This notion makes, to my mind, a vertical line of the world, a great chain of burning. The more accessible and universal view, held by Eckhart and by many peoples in various forms, is scarcely different from pantheism: that the world is immanation, that God is in the thing,

and eternally present here, if nowhere else. By these
lights the world is flattened on a horizontal plane,
singular, all here, crammed with heaven, and alone.
But I know that it is not alone, nor singular, nor all.
The notion of immanence needs a handle, and the
two ideas themselves need a link, so that life can
mean aught to the one, and Christ to the other.

For to immanence, to the heart, Christ is redundant
and all things are one. To emanance, to the mind,
Christ touches only the top, skims off only the top, as
it were, the souls of men, the wheat grains whole, and
lets the chaff fall where? To the world flat and
patently unredeemed; to the entire rest of the
universe, which is irrelevant and nonparticipant; to
time and matter unreal, and so unknowable, an
illusory, absurd, accidental, and overelaborate stage.

But if Holy the Firm is "underneath salts," if Holy
the Firm is matter at its dullest, Aristotle's *materia
prima,* absolute zero, and since Holy the Firm is in
touch with the Absolute at base, then the circle is
unbroken. And it is. Thought advances, and the
world creates itself, by the gradual positing of, and
belief in, a series of bright ideas. Time and space are

in touch with the Absolute at base. Eternity sockets twice into time and space curves, bound and bound by idea. Matter and spirit are of a piece but distinguishable; God has a stake guaranteed in all the world. And the universe is real and not a dream, not a manufacture of the senses; subject may know object, knowledge may proceed, and Holy the Firm is in short the philosopher's stone.

These are only ideas, by the single handful. Lines, lines, and their infinite points! Hold hands and crack the whip, and yank the Absolute out of there and into the light, God pale and astounded, spraying a spiral of salts and earths, God footloose and flung. And cry down the line to his passing white ear, "Old Sir! Do you hold space from buckling by a finger in its hole? O Old! Where is your other hand?" His right hand is clenching, calm, round the exploding left hand of Holy the Firm.

How can people think that artists seek a name? A name, like a face, is something you have when you're not alone. There is no such thing as an artist: there

is only the world, lit or unlit as the light allows.
When the candle is burning, who looks at the wick?
When the candle is out, who needs it? But the world
without light is wasteland and chaos, and a life
without sacrifice is abomination.

What can any artist set on fire but his world? What
can any people bring to the altar but all it has ever
owned in the thin towns or over the desolate plains?
What can an artist use but materials, such as they are?
What can he light but the short string of his gut, and
when that's burnt out, any muck ready to hand?

His face is flame like a seraph's, lighting the
kingdom of God for the people to see; his life goes
up in the works; his feet are waxen and salt. He is
holy and he is firm, spanning all the long gap with
the length of his love, in flawed imitation of Christ
on the cross stretched both ways unbroken and
thorned. So must the work be also, in touch with,
in touch with, in touch with; spanning the gap, from
here to eternity, home.

Hoopla! All that I see arches, and light arches
around it. The air churns out forces and lashes the
marveling land. A hundred times through the fields

and along the deep roads I've cried Holy. I see a hundred insects moving across the air, rising and falling. Chipped notes of birdsong descend from the trees, tuneful and broken; the notes pile about me like leaves. Why do these molded clouds make themselves overhead innocently changing, trailing their flat blue shadows up and down everything, and passing, and gone? Ladies and gentlemen! You are given insects, and birdsong, and a replenishing series of clouds. The air is buoyant and wholly transparent, scoured by grasses. The earth stuck through it is noisome, lighted, and salt. Who shall ascend into the hill of the Lord? or who shall stand in his holy place? "Whom shall I send," heard the first Isaiah, "and who will go for us?" And poor Isaiah, who happened to be standing there—and there was no one else—burst out, "Here am I; send me."

There is Julie Norwich. Julie Norwich is salted with fire. She is preserved like a salted fillet from all evil, baptized at birth into time and now into eternity, into the bladelike arms of God. For who will love her now, without a face, when women with faces abound, and people are so? People are reasoned, while God is mad. They love only beauty; who knows what God loves? Happy birthday, little one and wise: you got there early, the easy way. The world knew you before you knew the world. The gods in their boyish, brutal games bore you like a torch, a firebrand, recklessly over the heavens, to the glance of the one God, fathomless and mild, dissolving you into the sheets.

You might as well be a nun. You might as well be God's chaste bride, chased by plunderers to the high caves of solitude, to the heartless rooms empty of voices, and of warm limbs hooking your heart to the world. Look how he loves you! Are you bandaged now, or loose in a sterilized room? Wait till they hand you a mirror, if you can hold one, and know what it means. That skinlessness, that black shroud of flesh in strips on your skull, is your veil. There are two kinds of nun, out of the cloister or in. You can serve or you can sing, and wreck your heart in prayer, working the world's hard work. Forget whistling: you have no lips for that, or for kissing the face of a man or a child. Learn Latin, an it please my Lord, learn the foolish downward look called Custody of the Eyes.

And learn power, however sweet they call you, learn power, the smash of the holy once more, and signed by its name. Be victim to abruptness and seizures, events intercalated, swellings of heart. You'll climb trees. You won't be able to sleep, or need to, for the joy of it. Mornings, when light spreads over the pastures like wings, and fans a secret color into everything, and beats the trees senseless with beauty, so that you can't tell whether the beauty is *in* the trees—dazzling in cells like yellow sparks or green flashing waters—or *on* them—a transfiguring silver air charged with the wings' invisible motion; mornings, you won't be able to walk for the power of it: earth's too round. And by long and waking day—Sext, None, Vespers—when the grasses, living or dead, drowse while the sun reels, or lash in any wind, when sparrows hush and tides slack at the ebb, or flood up the beaches and cliffsides tangled with weed, and hay waits, and elsewhere people buy shoes —then you kneel, clattering with thoughts, ill, or some days erupting, some days holding the altar rail, gripping the brass-bolt altar rail, so you won't fly. Do you think I don't believe this? You have no idea, none. And nights? Nights after Compline under the ribs of Orion, nights in rooms at lamps or windows like moths? Nights you see Deneb, one-eyed over the trees; you vanish into the sheets, shrunken, your eyes bright as candles and as sightless, exhausted. Nights Murzim, Arcturus, Aldebaran in the Bull: You cry, My father, my father, the chariots of Israel, and the horsemen thereof! Held, held fast by love in the world like the moth in wax, your life a wick, your head on fire with prayer, held utterly, outside and in, you sleep alone, if you call that alone, you cry God.

Julie Norwich; I know. Surgeons will fix your face. This will all be a dream, an anecdote, something to tell your husband one night: I was burned. Or if you're scarred, you're scarred. People love the good not much less than the beautiful, and the happy as well, or even just the living, for the world of it all, and heart's home. You'll dress your own children, sticking their arms through the sleeves. Mornings you'll whistle, full of the pleasure of days, and afternoons this or that, and nights cry love. So live. I'll be the nun for you. I am now.